NOVEMBER

Ellen Jackson

Illustrated by
Pat DeWitt and Robin DeWitt

🏛 Charlesbridge

To Evalyn Rose
—E. J.

To Suzanne Diggs,
"notre Mamère" nous vous aimons
—P. D. & R. D.

Did You Know?

November is a quiet month, a time when the season's work is done and the earth rests. In November, much of life is stored underground in the seeds of plants and the eggs of insects. Ragged leaves drift into gutters and pile along roads.

The colors of November are earth tones—russet, bronze, and gold. The hills are brown, and bare tree branches look penciled against the sky.

November is a month of mists and frosts. One old superstition says that if there is thick ice on the pond in November, rain will be heavy in February: "If ice in November will bear a duck, / February weather all mire and muck!"

Thanksgiving comes toward the end of November in the United States, and turkeys and Indian corn are symbols of the month. Wild turkeys are very different from the tame birds we raise for food. They feed on insects, seeds, and berries. Though they prefer to walk, they can zip through the air at fifty-five miles per hour.

Pumpkins are another symbol of fall and Thanksgiving. The Pilgrims learned about pumpkins from the Wampanoag, a native people who taught them how to plant pumpkin seeds between rows of cornstalks in order to protect the growing plants from weeds.

The Wampanoag also showed the Pilgrims bitter-tasting red berries that we now call cranberries. The Pilgrims thought the pink flowers on the plants looked like the heads of cranes, so they called them crane berries.

In late fall, people think about the winter ahead and make a few last-minute repairs to their houses. They also rake leaves, fill the bird feeder, or play a game of touch football.

Indoor sports are popular in November when the weather is often cold and rainy. Some children and parents compete with one another in the fast-moving game of Ping-Pong. It is great fun to whack the ball and send it bouncing over the net, catching your opponent off guard. Ping-Pong, also called table tennis, is enjoyed in many countries. But it is particularly well liked in China, where children as young as four learn to play the game.

Gymnastics is an indoor sport that features breathtaking cartwheels, handsprings, and somersaults. Even young children can learn the basics of gymnastics. In the 1976 Olympics in Montreal, Canada, Nadia Comaneci was the first gymnast to receive a perfect score from the judges, earning a 10.00 in the uneven-bars event. She was only fourteen.

The November Birthstone

The birthstone for November is the topaz. This gem comes in every color of the rainbow. In ancient times, people thought the topaz got its power from the sun, and it was considered a symbol of strength. One uncut topaz from Brazil, currently in the collection of the American Museum of Natural History in New York City, weighs nearly six hundred pounds.

The November Flower

If you were born in November, your special flower is the chrysanthemum. Chrysanthemums have long been particularly admired in Asia. In 500 B.C., the philosopher Confucius wrote that the chrysanthemum "has its yellow glory." In China, the chrysanthemum was considered a symbol of long life and perfection. Chrysanthemum petals can be eaten and are sometimes added to soups and salads.

The November Zodiac

Scorpio, the scorpion, is the astrological sign for people with birthdays from October 24 to November 21. Scorpios are said to like puzzles of all kinds, and they make great detectives. They love Halloween, monster stories, and mysteries, and they can usually get what they want. A Scorpio is thought to be brave but can also be stubborn.

The sign for people born from November 22 to December 21 is Sagittarius, the archer. Those born under Sagittarius are thought to be happy-go-lucky, affectionate, and interested in philosophy and religion. A Sagittarius is always asking questions and is very honest. Sometimes, though, he or she can be a little clumsy.

The Calendar

November is the eleventh month of the year and has thirty days. In ancient Rome, the year began in March, not January. November was then the ninth month, and its name comes from the Latin word *novem*, which means "nine."

The rulers of ancient Rome changed the number of days in November from thirty to twenty-nine to thirty-one. Finally Augustus Caesar gave the month thirty days once and for all.

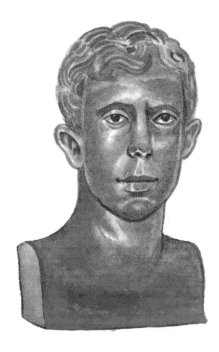

Sun, Sky, and Weather

In November, the dust of summer has been swept away, and the air is as clear as glass. The wind makes a haunting sound as it shuffles and reshuffles piles of dead leaves.

November's days are short and chilly. By five o'clock, it is nearly dark. In the city, the first flurry of snow catches people off guard. No one is ready to say good-bye to the mild weather.

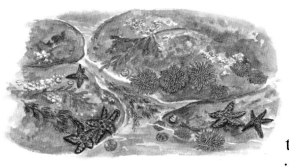

At the beaches,
tide pools churn
with life. November
is a good time to search for purple sea urchins and
comb the beach for shells washed up after a storm.

The Anglo-Saxons, who settled in Britain in the
fifth and sixth centuries, called November *Wind
monath* because it was a time of fierce winds. It was
also called *Blod monath*, or blood month, because
it was a time to slaughter animals for the coming
winter. The November full moon has been called
the beaver moon by some Native American peoples
of the Northeast because beavers gather food and
build their lodges
by its light.

Animals in November

Only a few insects and birds remain in the leafless November woods. The twitter and trill, drone and hum of summer are gone.

In late fall, a few animals go into a deep sleep called hibernation. True hibernators, such as woodchucks and bats, sleep so deeply that it is almost impossible to wake them up. Other animals, such as bears, are lighter sleepers.

When an animal hibernates, its heart rate and breathing slow down, and it lives off the fat its body has stored. Before hibernating, some insects and beetles bury themselves in mud or attach themselves to underwater plants. Frogs and water turtles burrow into the mud at the bottom of a pond or into the ground below the frost line.

Curled up into tight balls, chipmunks also hibernate through the winter. They sleep in nests made of grass or thistledown on top of piles of nuts and seeds. During the winter, they wake up from time to time to have a snack. A chipmunk's heart slows from two hundred beats a minute to just one or two beats a minute when it hibernates.

Many animals, especially insects, die in the late fall. If you look at soil under a microscope, you will find bits of wings, antennae, and other parts of insects mixed with dead plants, animal droppings, and earth. The decaying plants and animals enrich the soil so that new growth can begin in the spring.

In Nebraska, bobwhite quail prepare for the winter by finding brush cover near a source of food, such as a cornfield. When they roost, the birds form a tight circle with their tails pointed inward and their heads facing out. This helps keep each bird warm and safe from predators.

The chuckwalla is a large desert lizard that eats flowers, fruits, and leaves. In the fall, it crawls into a deep crack in a rock. If a predator finds it, the chuckwalla swallows air until it balloons in size, wedging itself into the crack so its enemy cannot pull it out.

If you live near a park, you might notice that squirrels' tails are bigger and bushier than they were in the summer. Squirrels use their tails for blankets, and they need an extra warm blanket when the weather gets cold!

Plants in November

In the woods, most of the fall flowers have faded, but dandelions and asters are still in bloom. The leaves and twigs that fell in late October have formed a mat on the forest floor. This mat will provide winter shelter for tiny animals and insect eggs. After the first rains, bacteria, algae, earthworms, and insects will begin to recycle the dead vegetation.

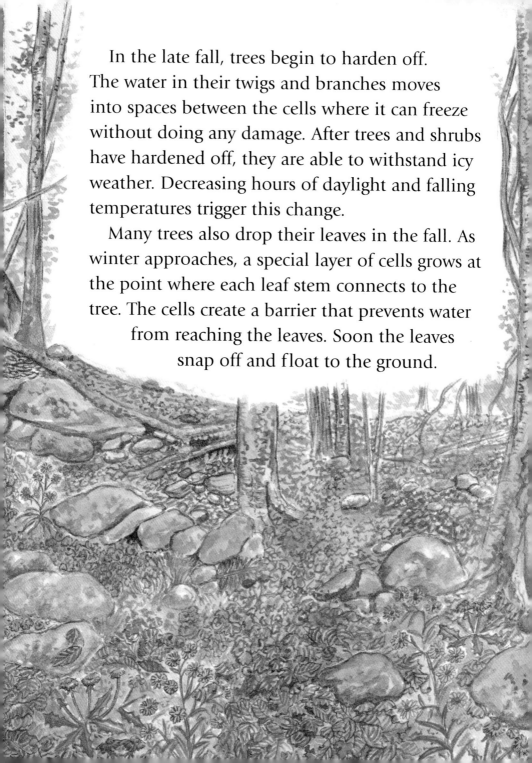

In the late fall, trees begin to harden off. The water in their twigs and branches moves into spaces between the cells where it can freeze without doing any damage. After trees and shrubs have hardened off, they are able to withstand icy weather. Decreasing hours of daylight and falling temperatures trigger this change.

Many trees also drop their leaves in the fall. As winter approaches, a special layer of cells grows at the point where each leaf stem connects to the tree. The cells create a barrier that prevents water from reaching the leaves. Soon the leaves snap off and float to the ground.

On the prairie, all that is left of the wildflowers of summer are a few dried stalks with seedless heads. Only the downy gentian is still in flower. It opens its blossoms if the days are bright and sunny.

In November, tumbleweeds break off at the stem and begin to roll across the desert. A tumbleweed looks like a huge ball of dead branches. As tumbleweeds roll along, their seeds scatter across the ground.

Special Days

Election Day

In the United States, election day falls on the first Tuesday after the first Monday in November. Many state, local, and congressional elections are held on this day. Every four years, the citizens of the United States vote for a new president.

Two hundred years ago, only white male landowners were allowed to vote in national elections. African American men were given the vote in 1870, and women won the same right in 1920. In 1971, the Twenty-sixth Amendment to the United States Constitution made the voting age eighteen nationwide.

Veterans Day

Veterans Day is celebrated on November 11 to honor all those who have served in the armed forces of the United States. Veterans Day was originally called Armistice Day. At the end of World War I, an armistice, or truce, was signed between the warring countries at eleven o'clock on the eleventh day of the eleventh month. Everyone hoped there would never be such a terrible war again.

In 1938, the United States Congress made Armistice Day a national holiday dedicated to "the cause of world peace." In 1954, the name of the day was changed to Veterans Day to honor veterans of all wars.

Thanksgiving

The fourth Thursday in November is Thanksgiving Day in the United States. In 1621, the Pilgrims who settled Plimoth Colony were grateful for their harvest and for the help of the Wampanoag. The Wampanoag had told them which crops would do well in the new land. The Pilgrims decided to hold a feast and invite their new friends. About fifty Pilgrims and ninety Wampanoag took part in the three-day celebration. Wild turkey, deer, and goose were served.

In 1863, President Abraham Lincoln made Thanksgiving an official annual holiday in the United States. Today most Americans celebrate Thanksgiving with a dinner of turkey, potatoes, cranberries, and pumpkin pie.

Famous November Events

On November 19, 1863, President Abraham Lincoln gave a speech to dedicate a new national cemetery at Gettysburg, Pennsylvania. The Battle of Gettysburg, which began on July 1, 1863, was one of the bloodiest battles of the American Civil War. More than fifty thousand Confederate and Union soldiers were killed or wounded. President Lincoln's Gettysburg Address is one of the most famous speeches in history.

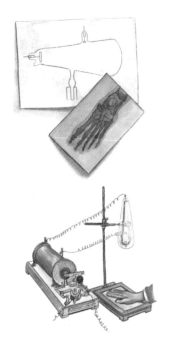

On November 8, 1895, physicist Wilhelm Conrad Roentgen discovered X rays when he noticed that invisible rays from a cathode-ray tube caused a piece of paper coated with chemicals to glow with light. His observations led to the discovery of radioactivity and the invention of new medical devices, such as X-ray machines.

On November 3, 1957, the Soviet Union launched *Sputnik II*, the second man-made satellite to go into orbit around the earth. The satellite was nicknamed Muttnik by the American press because it carried the first animal to fly in outer space, a dog named Laika. While Laika did not survive the trip, *Sputnik II* helped pave the way for human exploration of space.

On November 22, 1963, John F. Kennedy, the thirty-fifth president of the United States, was killed by an assassin's bullet in Dallas, Texas. President Kennedy fought for the rights of the poor, the rights of minorities, and the right to quality education.

Birthdays

Many famous people were born in November.

Frontiersman, military officer, and explorer.

Polish chemist, physicist, and winner of the Nobel Prize in chemistry for her discovery of radium.

Mathematician, astronomer, and surveyor who helped plan the construction of Washington, D.C.

American artist, noted for her paintings of desert scenes and flowers.

Wilma Mankiller

November 18, 1945

First woman principal
chief of the Cherokee
Nation.

Indira Gandhi

November 19, 1917

First woman prime
minister of India.

Adolfo Pérez Esquivel

November 26, 1931

Sculptor, architect, and
Argentine human-rights
activist. Winner of the
1980 Nobel Peace Prize.

Bruce Lee

November 27, 1940

Martial-arts expert and
actor, who starred in the
television series *The
Green Hornet* and the
film *Enter the Dragon*.

Louisa May Alcott

November 29, 1832

Author of books for adults
and children. Her most
famous works are *Little
Women* and *Little Men*.

Winston Churchill

November 30, 1874

British statesman and
prime minister of
England during World
War II.

A November Story

Thirty children set off to explore the New World with their parents and guardians when the *Mayflower* sailed for America on September 5, 1620. All of these children were expected to pitch in and help with the work. But they were not all obedient and well behaved. John and Francis Billington were two young Pilgrim boys who often got into trouble. During the voyage, one of them fired a gun near a powder keg and almost blew up the ship.

After the Pilgrims settled at Plimoth, the brothers had many adventures. Once Francis climbed a tall tree and saw water in the distance. He ran home and announced to everyone that he had discovered the Pacific Ocean. He had actually discovered a big pond. The Pilgrims named it Billington's Sea in his honor, and it is still called that today.

One summer day, John Billington wandered into the woods and got lost. For five days, the Pilgrims searched for him. Everyone was worried. Finally Wampanoag chief Massasoit sent word from Nauset, on Cape Cod, that they had found the boy and he was safe.

A party of Pilgrims sailed to Nauset, where they were met by a party of one hundred Wampanoag. The chief was carrying John, who was loaded down with necklaces of beads and shells. Because of a lost boy, the settlers and the Wampanoag began a long period of friendship.

AUTHOR'S NOTE

This book gives an overview of the month of November in North America. But nature does not follow a strict schedule. The mating and migration of animals, the blooming of plants, and other natural events vary from year to year, or occur earlier or later in different places.

The zodiac sections of this book are included just for fun as part of the folklore of the month and should not be taken as accurate descriptions of any real people.

The November story was adapted from several sources, including *Turkeys, Pilgrims, and Indian Corn* by Edna Barth. (New York: Clarion Books, 1975.)

Text copyright © 2002 by Ellen Jackson
Illustrations copyright © 2002
  by Pat DeWitt and Robin DeWitt
All rights reserved, including the right of
  reproduction in whole or in part in any form.

Published by Charlesbridge Publishing
85 Main Street, Watertown, MA 02472
(617) 926-0329
www.charlesbridge.com

Illustrations done in watercolor on Arches
  hot-press paper
Display type and text type set in Giovanni
Color separations made by Sung In Printing,
  South Korea
Printed and bound by Sung In Printing,
  South Korea
Production supervision by Brian G. Walker
Designed by Diane M. Earley

**Library of Congress
Cataloging-in-Publication Data**

Jackson, Ellen B., 1943-
    November/Ellen Jackson; illustrated by
  Pat DeWitt and Robin DeWitt.
    p. cm.—(It happens in the month of)
  ISBN 0-88106-927-2 (hardcover)
  1. November—Folklore. 2. November—
  Juvenile literature. [1. November.] I. DeWitt,
  Pat, ill. II. DeWitt, Robin, ill. III. Title.

GR930.J34   2002
398'.33—dc21   2001028265

Printed in South Korea
10 9 8 7 6 5 4 3 2 1